For Stephen

also by Posy Simmonds

FRED
LULU AND THE FLYING BABIES

First published 1990
© Posy Simmonds 1990
Jonathan Cape Ltd, 20 Vauxhall Bridge Road,
London SW1V 2SA

A CIP catalogue record for this book
is available from the British Library

ISBN 0-224-02759-X

Printed in Italy by
Arti Grafiche Motta S.p.A. Milan

POSY SIMMONDS

THE CHOCOLATE WEDDING

JONATHAN CAPE

LONDON

Lulu is going to be a bridesmaid in a silvery pink dress....

Her Aunt Carrie is going to be a bride in a long white one. *Everyone* at Lulu's school knows this.

Lulu will be staying at her grandparents' house for the wedding....

I'm allowed to stay up really **LATE**!

...'Cos there'll be a big party...

..and a **GI-NORMOUS** wedding cake!

It's got a sugar bride and husband on top......

And it's got **THREE** floors! It's taller than Mrs Clarke!

You fibber!

On the evening before the wedding, Lulu, her mother and father and her little brother, Willy, drive to Granny and Grandpa's house........

Hallo, Lulu!

Hallo, Granny!

All the grown-ups are busy moving furniture and preparing food for the wedding party.....

Lulu and Willy go in the dining room. The wedding cake sits on a table covered in a long, white cloth. It looks much smaller today....not nearly as big as Mrs Clarke.

Lulu hides in a corner, near the radiator.

Inside her case are all the things she and Willy have been given for Easter: chocolate eggs, chocolate money, six chocolate soldiers and six chocolate kittens.....

Lulu eats three chocolate kittens and sixteen eggs.

Some of the eggs have insides she doesn't like.

Eeuch!

She spits these out.... and hides them under the radiator.

yuk!

Lulu always puts things she doesn't like behind radiators. There's already a bit of beetroot from supper...and a biscuit she got tired of.

Cake!

Man!

Lady!

Willy? What you doing?

No!

Will-ee?

What you eating? ...Show me!

No!

Elaahh!

Owh, NO!

There aren't enough beds for everyone at Granny's house. Lulu is sleeping on the sofa.....

It's the next day and everyone is ready to go to the church for the wedding, except Lulu. She was very sick in the night. She still feels ill.....

You keep nice and warm...and we'll be back very soon

Jenny from next door...

...and the ladies doing the waitressing will all keep an eye on you.

Lulu watches Aunt Carrie get into the wedding car. It's not a silver carriage. It's Grandpa's car, with white ribbons on it.

sniff!

There, Lulu...have a little snooze.....

BOO-HOO!

BOOo-HOOo!

?

This is her shoe?

Yes, her sweet little shoe...oh, she's SO, SO **sweet**!

Mmm! She **is** sweet...SUGAR!

NO! Don't **LICK** it!!!

Ooh!

Ooh!

Ooh!

Ooh!

Ooh!

!!

WHAT happened!

I've gone all **WEENY**!

Oh! I **TOLD** you not to **LICK** it!!

Oh DEAR!

Please...can I come in?

NO!

BUZZ OFF!

If I give you some money, can I...?

No..we don't like money!

But it's **CHOCOLATE** money......*look!*

Hm

Mmm!

Hey, Chief! This is *good stuff!*

How much is there? Get her to count it...

Oh...I'm not very good at counting

I AM!

I'll help you!

14

15

Try a bit, Chief...

Ssh!

FOLLOW ME!

Oh!

DID you?

Mum, I just fell off the top of the wedding cake....!

Let's wash..and put your dress on, shall we?

Feeling better, Lulu?

Mum! I dreamt I found the **sugar bride!**

Poor bride! Naughty Willy ate her, didn't he?

No, he didn't!

I dreamt he threw her on the floor!

P'raps he did ...let's go and see.

To Sweety-pie
and Sweety-poo!